GOLFSPEAK

The Art of Inane Golfing Commentary

Jack J. Bainter

TABLE OF CONTENTS

PREFACE

Every week millions of people worldwide watch televised golf tournaments. These fans have a right to expect reporting that is accurate, well spoken, and professional in presentation. Some sports announcers are highly talented, some adequately talented, and the remainder provide the material for this book.

I am not privy to the pay stubs of those sportscasters, but feel confident assuming that, on the whole, they are a very well paid group. Therefore, shouldn't those announcers be held to standards of proper grammar and broadcast delivery? I think they should. Unfortunately, many of those microphone jocks speak what I call *sportspeak,* or in the case of golf announcers, *golfspeak.*

About 20 years ago I was watching a golf match on television and noticed the announcer referring repeatedly to drives, chips, putts, etc. as great *golf* shots. Wasn't I to assume that since I had been watching the match for two hours that the shots I was seeing were *golf* shots? This led me to be mindful of other broadcasts whereupon

I discovered reporting faux pas after faux pas. Over the years I jotted down scores of such comments and present many of them in this book. Each comment was actually stated on the air. Some are worthy of a laugh, some a groan, some a tear, and all a careful reflection. Each announcer's comment is followed by my own reaction.

CHAPTER ONE

Perfect Shots

Some golf announcers for both women's and men's tournaments make wild stabs at being cutesy and dramatic. Contrary to what these announcers and television producers believe, a little dead air time may be preferable to meaningless babble. An old New England proverb is to "say nothing unless you can improve on silence." Sportscasters would do well to adhere to that concept. They should just report the play in straightforward language that wouldn't have Noah Webster turning over in his grave.

It seems that golf announcers are enamored with the words *"safely"* and *"perfect."* We viewers are repeatedly reminded that players are "safely on" and "safely in." Never have I heard that a player is unsafely on or unsafely in. One is either on the putting surface or not, and is either in the hole or not.

I cannot count the number of *"perfect"* shots I have heard golf announcers claim. This shot description is, I believe, more prevalent during women's tournament broadcasts, but is a common comment during men's matches as well. Perhaps the classic statement was from a Skins Game broadcast during which the four players teed off and the announcer declared "all four players are in perfect position." How could there be four perfect drives when they each landed in a different position on the fairway? Here follows further "perfect" statements made.

1. "He hit that putt perfectly; just didn't read it right."

    How can that be?

2. "Absolutely diabolically perfect."

    A little drama here?

3. "You couldn't have walked four drives out here more perfectly than these."

> This was a different tournament than the one mentioned in the preface about the four Skins Game players. But, it may have been the same announcer.

4. "If you were going to leave the ball in a perfect position to putt from, that's where you'd want it."

> Bear in mind that the ball stopped 20 feet from the hole. Wouldn't an inch from the hole have been a nearer perfect putting position?

5. "You couldn't hand place it any better."

The ball was a foot off the fairway and about 100 yards from the green. I don't want that announcer placing my golf balls.

6. "That is perfect and long."

Makes you wonder if the shot would have been considered perfect if it wasn't long.

7. "He has driven his ball to the most perfect spot you could hit it."

   I'm glad it wasn't to the least perfect spot.

8. "Rocky's put it out absolutely perfectly."

   Not just perfectly, but absolutely so.

9. "That's absolutely perfect. Absolutely perfect."

    Do you get the point or do you need a third reminder that the shot was absolutely perfect?

10. "Eight feet short of the pin. Just perfect."

    What would it have been if two feet short?

11. "Three perfect tee shots."
    Here we go again.

12. "Couldn't draw it on a piece of paper any better than that shot there."
    The ball was still several yards from the hole.

13. "Not as long as you'd like it to be, but it's in perfect shape."

   What would it be if it had been as long as you'd like it?

14. "Absolutely perfect. Exact same putt; about a foot shorter."

   Exact same putt, but a foot different in distance. Interesting definition of *"exact same."* Also, if it is the same, it has to be exact same, or is there an inexact same?

15. "How perfect was that golf shot?"

    Mind you, the golfer missed the hole by about 15 feet.

16. "You can't do any better than that."

    This said as golfer missed his putt.

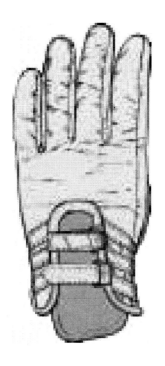

CHAPTER TWO

Men's Golf

Now, here are more men's golf pronouncements that must have referred to less than perfect shots.

17. "I don't know how he missed."
    Could it be that he hit it wrong?

18. "Just as soon as he hit it, it took off."
    Do tell.

19.   "This hole has treated him very scurvily."
      Glad it wasn't shabbily too.

20.   "If you had to play John Daly on this hole
      the rest of your life, nobody would win."
      Now just what does that mean?

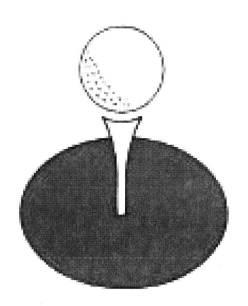

21. "That was a magnificent shot. Never mind the result."

    I reckon that if the results didn't matter, I may have made a few magnificent shots.

22. "That makes the hole a lot shorter."

    I suggest that if the reference is to the ball flight, the next shot might be a shorter distance, but the hole hasn't moved. Maybe he used the ladies' tee, eh?

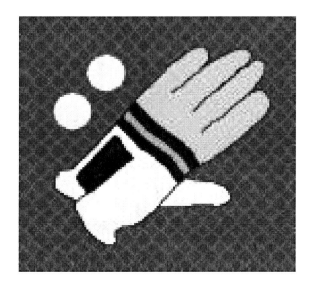

23. "It just ran out of real estate."

    The ball stopped one ball rotation short of the hole. Perhaps there were about two inches too much real estate. This is a prime example of the announcer trying to be overly cute.

24. "I never see Tiger leave it short very often."

    Does the announcer mean *never* or *not often!* Can't have it both ways.

25. "I'm sure he's looking at the leader board and wants to climb more."

    This player was one stroke off the lead. Why wouldn't he want to move up the leader board?

26. "That was too good a putt not to go in."

    How could that be? Besides, the putt missed the hole by a foot.

27.　"He's got the better part of 50 feet."

Does that mean nearly 50 feet or 25 feet and one inch?

28.　"It's a chance to get that shot back."

Dropping a shot on an earlier hole is not retractable. That stroke is gone forever. A birdie on a subsequent hole does not get back a lost stroke.

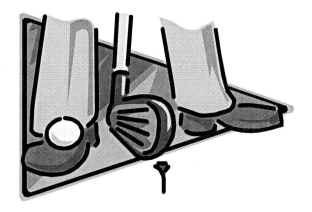

29. "The whole field would putt this, but not Raymond Floyd."

Isn't Raymond Floyd part of the field?

30. "That could have gone in just as easily as it stayed out."

Now, I doubt that or it would have gone in.

31. "He had the exact same putt."

Must have been the same announcer from item 14 above. Will it never end? See number 32 below.

32. "Kirk Triplett hit the exact same shot... couldn't be more identical."

Not just identical, but more identical. At least it wasn't absolutely identical. But, it was still "exact same."

33. "The lie will dictate what club to use here."
     Isn't that always the case?

34. "Club selection here is a must."
     Club selection is always a must since kicking the ball is frowned upon.

35.   "If he'd made a couple more putts on the front nine, he would have posted a much lower score."

Lower maybe, but only by two strokes.

36.   "He takes the club back in one piece."

Well, well. I'm glad he didn't opt to take the club back in multiple pieces. That would have made for an awkward shot.

37. "He played the right shot, but did not hit it far enough."

    Sounds like it wasn't quite the right shot.

38. "He hasn't made any putts all day. He needs to make one now."

    Please tell me, if he has made no putts, how has he made it to the 17th green? Maybe 16 chips into the hole?

39. "He has been just spotless in his play."

This player had made five birdies and one bogie in 15 holes. Making a bogie hardly qualifies as spotless play, though five birdies in 15 holes seem noteworthy. It would be for me.

40. "There are players here from every corner of the globe."

I have never seen a globe with corners.

41.   "If you hit it, you'll make it."

Said as the putt went six inches past the hole.

42.   "You can't just go up and nonchalant the ball in the hole."

What kind of verbiage is that?

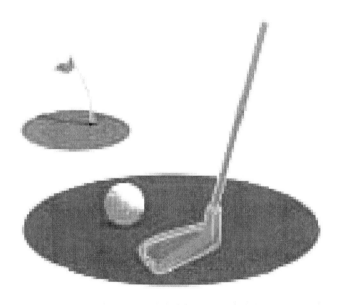

43. "Get the ball rolling end over end as soon as possible."

     Just where is the end of a golf ball, or does this guy play golf using a football?

44. "He's direly in need of some kind of putt."

     Isn't every golfer in need of some kind of putt? Hasn't the golfer hit some kinds of putts already?

45. "It just runs out of speed."

    Every golf shot in the world runs out of speed somewhere.

46. "That's exactly about what he has played."

    I suppose an *exactly about* is the best kind *of about*, eh?

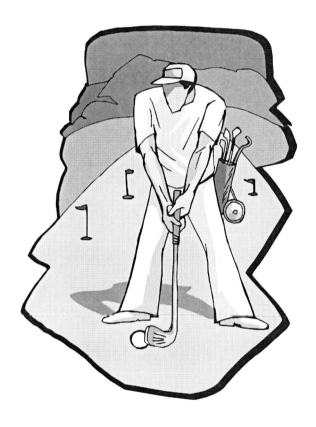

47. "You can not hit the flag stick more dead center than that was."

    I reckon the center of a flag stick is the center and dead center is dead center, but hitting more dead center is commendable.

48. "He snatches a par away from a sure bogey."

    Wow, what a magician.

49. "Except for a double bogie on the 15th yesterday, he would be further up the leader board."

And, except for making fewer birdies, he would be yet further up the leader board.

50. "He has a chip he can play any of two ways."

So, any of two ways adds intrigue, I bet.

51. "Beautiful shot. Right where you want it."

    The ball stopped about 15 feet left of the pin. That's hardly where I would want it.

52. "This is a colossal performance here in a first Masters."

    I bet he will never again match his *colossal* performance.

53. "He missed the green rather comprehensively."

    Is that good or bad? Or, just comprehensive?

54. "That was like a different guy played the hole than everybody else."

    Hey, I hope he was a different person than everybody else.

55. "You just have to play it like a semi-bunker shot."

Now, just what is a semi-bunker shot like?

56. "That would have gone in if he'd have hit it."

What can I say? You just have to hit the ball to get it in the hole.

57. "On the same exact hole."

     Here we go again with the same exact faux pas.

58. "It hit the back left center of the hole."

     Since golf holes are circular, just where is "left center?"

59. "He's standing across his shadow."

Then why doesn't he move? Do you suppose he was putting across his shadow?

60. "He hit a wonderful shot, but he pulled it."

Maybe it wasn't so wonderful.

61. "It was a better shot than it ended up."

    Come on now. No shot is any better than it ends up.

62. "No one will do better than that out of that bunker."

    Since the golfer failed to hit the hole, I imagine that it would be possible for someone to do better.

63.   "Will that filter back?"

How does a golf ball filter?

64.   "It is excruciatingly quiet now."

Folks, I reckon that that is the Nth degree of quiet.

65. "His normally dependable putter simply let him down."

Yes, I guess the putter just decided to not do its expected job that particular day. Couldn't have been how the putter was used that resulted in poor putting.

66. "Performed a miracle to stay out of the hole."

With balls that perform miracles, its no wonder the professionals are normally so good, unless some miracles are misdirected.

67. "Just about where you want to hit it as a player."

Where would you want to hit if you weren't a player.

68. "That's as good as a birdie."

Baloney. No par is as good as a birdie.

69.	"Its easy to see that the green surfaces are in great condition today. That ball rolled all the way to the hole."

Could the distance of the roll have been influenced by the force of the putt? Incidentally, the putt the announcer was reporting stopped six inches short of the hole.

70.	"That's as well as he could play this shot, and still ended up 10 feet."

I just doubt whether that was as well as the golfer could have played the shot.

71.   "He needs to get a putt in the hole though somehow."

Isn't that always the case?

72.   "Every one of these holes will have its own trouble today."

Don't you think it is players who have troubles, not the holes?

73. "There was nothing wrong with that putt."

Guess what. It missed the hole. Maybe something was wrong with the putt.

74. "He doesn't need problems like that, does he?"

What kind of problems does he need then?

75. "That is a good smart shot."

    This was said after the golfer had pitched into the crowd.

76. "There is simply no limit to what this young man can do."

    Now there is a bold statement. I reckon he could cure cancer, stop wars, extinguish hunger, and solve the AIDS problem. Why does he not branch out beyond golf?

CHAPTER THREE

Women's Golf

77. "There just isn't any way to get it to the hole from down there."

How about a long putt or accurate chip?

78. "It really hurts your score; those three-putts."

How astute! This was said in reference to a player having to take three putts to finish three different holes on the front nine.

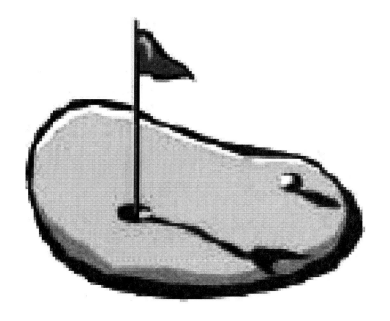

79.   "We haven't seen too many putts holed on this green."

Hmm. Players cannot proceed to the next hole unless they hole their putts on the current hole they are playing.

80.   "Sometimes the good Lord doesn't give everybody everything."

Surprise, surprise. Who thought everybody got everything?

81. "She's the third player in this pairing."

    Well, well, three makes a pair. I didn't know that.

82. "If she hits it dead center, it's going in." Said in reference to a putt.

    I reckon this is always true unless it is hit too hard or a chipmunk rears its head in the hole and deflects the ball.

83. "You will never see her do that very often."

    I bet that's true.

84. "Speed is the entire key here."

    As if direction counts for nothing.

85. "Didn't miss a fairway on Friday, and can't seem to hit a fairway today when it counts."

    A stroke entered on the scorecard counts the same regardless of the day of the tournament, doesn't it?

86. "Betsy King's got the exact putt she wants. It's almost eight feet."

    Could it be that a one-foot putt would be more desirable than one at eight feet?

87.　"You couldn't put it in a better spot."

　　This was said when the tee shot was left 12 yards short of the green. Now really!

88.　"You couldn't come down here and place it in a better position."

　　And the shot stopped five feet short of the hole.

89.   "How does it feel winning four consecutive tournaments in a row?"

   As opposed to winning consecutive tournaments not in a row.

90.   "They're just similar enough that they're entirely different."

   This reference to certain golf holes just leaves me scratching my head.

91. "Can't play it any better than that."

    Another comment about a shot that stopped short of the hole; this one five or six feet short.

92. "You don't need to commentate when..."

    Now there is a rarely used word.

93.   "She hit it right where she meant to...it just never moved."

Golf announcers and players attach their own meaning to the word *move*. Even so, if she hit it where she meant to, wouldn't it be where she wanted it to be?

94.   "She couldn't have hand-placed it any better."

Come now, it wasn't even on the green.

95. "You simply don't make putts like that."

    This was said after the player made a putt.

96. "She's trying to get back to basic fundamentals."

    That ought to help her game. Those basic fundamentals are the most helpful kind.

97. "...difficult to putt the greens."

    Where else should the players putt?

98. "She is six months pregnant. She has one daughter four years old. I'm not sure she knows the sex of it"

    Hey, let's hope she figures it out before the child starts school. After four years, she ought to have gotten some clues.

99. "There's nothing worse than having a six on your scorecard."

   I guess that if it appears one is about to make a six, it would be wise to deliberately miss a shot so a seven could be the score.

100. "That ball had a chance to go in the hole from all sides."

   What an interesting golfing technique. I bet this is true for very few golfers.

Good golfing. Have an incredibly perfect game